NO FEAR FORAGING

A Field Guide to the Most Common
Edible & Medicinal Plants in the USA.

Jeromie Jackson

CONTENTS

	Acknowledgments	Pg 4
	Introduction	Pg **5**
1	Cattail	Pg 6
2	Chickweed	Pg 8
3	Clover	Pg 9
4	Curly Dock	Pg 10
5	Dandelion	Pg 11
6	Lambsquarters	Pg 12
7	Mallow	Pg 13
8	Mullein	Pg 14
9	Mustard	Pg 15
10	Oak	Pg 16
11	Pine	Pg 18
12	Plantain	Pg 19
13	Purslane	Pg 20
14	Rose	Pg 21
15	Stinging Nettle	Pg 22
16	Stork's Bill	Pg 24
17	Sunflower	Pg 25
18	Thistle	Pg 26
19	Willow	Pg 27
20	Yarrow	Pg 28
21	Definitions	Pg 29

ACKNOWLEFDGMENTS

I would like to acknowledge Christopher Nyerges, Chris Morasky, Pascal Baudar, Mia Wasilevich, Dave Canterbury, and the California Native Plant Society for their assistance in the development of this book. Without the relationships I have built over the years, this book would not have been possible.

Christopher Nyerges has been my primary plant mentor through both his writings and the times we have shared together. My favorite book is "Guide to Wild Foods and Useful Plants." Pascal Baudar and Mia Wasilevich have inspired me with beautiful dishes and unique approaches to food preparation. Pascal wrote an exceptional book enitled "The New Wildcrafted Cuisine: Exploring the Exotic Gastronomy of Local Terroir." Mia Wasilevich's book, "Ugly Little Greens", is another fantastic resource for creating beautiful and tasty dishes from the landscape.

Dave Canterbury has been an important source for much of my bushcraft and self-reliance skills. Chris Morasky has dramatically impacted my perspective on what it means to be comfortable outdoors, to be sensitive to what is occurring around me and to be present in the landscape. My father, Ed Jackson, took us camping, hunting, fishing shooting off rockets and all things outdoors. The time in the bush provided the foundation for my appreciation of being in the dirt. My daughter, Autumn, has been my forager, sieu chef and taster of many of the dishes and drinks we've made. Our outdoor foraging activities and time in the kitchen have brought us closer together and given her a deeper appreciation for nature.

Thank you all for sharing your time, knowledge and passion for the outdoors.

INTRODUCTION

This book is a field guide of the most common plants found throughout the United States. When traveling outside of the southwest, I often found myself lost when it came to what plants I could seek to use in a given territory. This book is based on my research documenting where plants are found in the United States based on the USDA Flora Database (www.plantsusa.gov).

Once the top-20 plants were identified, I studied many sources, both native and contemporary, to document how people can use the plants. Books often refer to plant edibility or medicinal values, yet neglect to specify what parts of the plant to use and recommended preparation methods. I have highlighted these areas in the field guide.

For those new to learning about plants, I highly recommend asking local experts who teach about the plants in your area. Many areas have local botanists, ethnobotanists and others who are willing to share their knowledge. By far the quickest way I expanded my knowledge was by walking outdoors with Christopher Nyerges & Chris Morasky. I would take notes and use as many senses as possible to learn about the plant. In California, I also recommend Blue Winds School of Botanical Studies where Tellur Fenner travels around the west studying and teaching.

Plants often contain lots many of vitamins and minerals, yet lack calories and fats needed to sustain our bodies. Refer to the definitions of terms I've used on page 29. Compiled in this book, is the nutritional values of each of the plants documented. Long-term survival requires positive calorie consumption. I have identified calorie dense plants with a symbol at the top-right of the page to enable readers to focus on maintaining energy in long-term scenarios.

1. Cattail

Family: Typhaceae	Common Family: Cattail
Genus: Typha L.	Common Genus: Cattail
Species: Typha latifolia	

IDENTIFICATION:
Cattails have long, slender, flat leaves that are "D" shaped when cut in half. Tall stalks grow with the familiar "hot dog on a stick" at the top. When the plant cut in half, there are concentric rings as opposed to the fan-shaped, poison iris.

EDIBLE: Many parts of the cattail are edible. Early in the season, above the female flower, the male counterpart grows. Once it opens, it will be covered in a bright yellow pollen that can be easily collected and used as a flour. The female portion, when green and closed, can be cooked and eaten like corn-on-the-cob. Young shoots can be eaten, as well as the inner white shoots from the base of the plant. The rhizomes (horizontal growing roots) can also be eaten. Be cautious of the water from which they are harvested. Cooking is generally recommended. These rhizomes are full of starches that can be roasted to convert to sugars and contain approximately 6%- 8% protein and 80% carbohydrates.

MEDICINAL:

Part	Preparation	Application	Usage
Pollen & Rhizomes	None	Topical	Bleeding
Rhizomes	Dried and Pulverized	Ingested	Abdominal Cramps
Roots	Flour/Paste	Ingested	Kidney Stones
Mucilaginous Substance at Base of Leaves	None	Topical	Burns and Dermatological Aid
Fuzz From Female	None	Topical	Wound Covering & Anti-Chafing

UTILITARIAN: The leaves can be braided to make cordage, straps and baskets. I've used it successfully on primitive backpacks and similar projects. Leaves can also be woven to make sandals and skirts. It is best to dry them in a dark, cool place. They should be slightly rehydrated before braiding. Mats can be easily made to help mitigate conductive heat loss at night. The stems, both the female and male components, grow on the stalk. The stalks make great chopsticks. The Kumeyaay Indians used them to make a shelter called an Ewa that resembled a dome made of willow framing and cattail shingles. Pollen can also be used for face painting. Down from the female portion can be used for the back of blowgun darts. Entire darts can be made from dry stalks for small birds. The down provides good insulation and is a great flash-tinder to start fires. I have also had good success using the stalks as hand-drill spindles for a friction fire. Charred, whole female portions make a great carrier for an ember should you need to move camp.

CAUTION: Poison Iris and Cattails often grow next to each other. When harvesting, ensure you are foraging from the correct plant. Cattails are cylindrical at the base, and a single leaf is "D" shaped when cut in half. Iris leaves are fan shaped and do not have cylindrical rings.

2. Chickweed

Family: Caryophyllaceae	Common Family: Pink
Genus: Stellaria L.	Common Genus: Chickweed
Species: Stellaria media	

IDENTIFICATION:

Chickweed is a short, clumping plant. It has thin stems, opposite, oval-shaped leaves and tiny white flowers with 5 petals that are so deeply lobed it may look like 10. Hairs grow on the stems and change direction at the nodes. In 1 cup of Chickweed, there is 42 grams of protein, 21,726 grams of carbohydrates and 10,200mg of Vitamin A.

EDIBLE: All parts of the plant are edible raw or cooked.

MEDICINAL:

Part	Preparation	Application	Usage
Leaves	Decoction	Wash	Sore Eyes
Leaves	Poultice	Topical	Relieve Skin Irritations

UTILITARIAN: None Known

CAUTION: There is a look-a-like called Spurge. You may hear, "Spurge will make you purge." The key identifier is Spurge has a milky sap whereas Chickweed does not.

3. Clover

Family: Faboideae	Common Family: Pea
Genus: Trifolium L.	Common Genus: Clover
Species: Trifolium repens	

IDENTIFICATION:

The clover has 3-parted leaves that exhibit a moon-shaped watermark. Flowers are small and white or pink. The blooms are circular and often resemble a ball. Clover contains approximately 23% protein.

EDIBLE: Leaves, seeds and flowers can be eaten raw or cooked.

MEDICINAL:

Part	Preparation	Application	Usage
Leaves	Poultice	Topical	Hemostatic

UTILITARIAN: None Known

CAUTION: None Known

4. Curly Dock

Family: Polygonaceae	Common Family: Buckwheat
Genus: Rumex L.	Common Genus: Dock
Species: Rumex crispus L.	

IDENTIFICATION:

Curly Dock grows as a rosette of wavy leaves around a central crown with broad simple leaves. If you see blotches on the leaves, they are probably too mature to be tasty to eat. Seeds densely grow on the stalk and can quickly yield a significant amount of food. In 1 cup of leaves, there is approximately 4.5 grams of protein, 12.3 grams of carbohydrates.

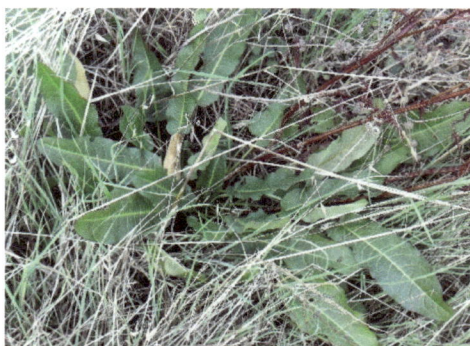

EDIBLE: Leaves are best early in season due to the oxalic acid that increases as the plant matures. It is recommended to place the leaves in hot water and change the water a time or 2, if needed, to reduce the acid. The seeds can also be harvested in large quantities quickly and make good flour for crackers. Dock contains significant amounts of vitamin A, C and potassium. Roasted seeds have been used as a coffee substitute.

MEDICINAL:

Part	Preparation	Application	Usage
Roots	Poultice	Topical	Swelling & Skin Problems
Roots	Tea	Ingested	Antidiarrheal
Leaves	Poultice	Topical	Draw out Puss, Hemorrhoids
Leaves	Cooked	Ingested	Blood Purifier, Liver Aid, Cramps, Abdominal Pain, & Kidney Problems
Seeds	Boiled	Ingested	Diarrhea

UTILITARIAN: The yellow leaves and stems are used to make a dye.

CAUTION: Eat in moderation due to the acids found in the plant.

5. Dandelion

Family: Asteraceae	Common Family: Aster
Genus: Taraxacum	Common Genus: Dandelion
Species: Taraxacum officinale	

IDENTIFICATION:

Dandelion is generally easy to identify due to its basal rosette shape, deeply lobed and hairless leaves, milky sap, familiar flower, and seed head that is often seen being blown into the wind.

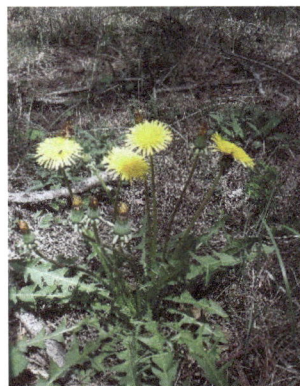

EDIBLE:

All parts of the Dandelion are edible, raw or cooked. The roots can be roasted to make a coffee substitute or extender. The flowers are often used to make wine. Dandelions are a good source of Vitamins A, C, E and K as well as calcium, iron, sodium, and potassium. In 100g of Dandelion greens, there are 4.20g of protein, 11600 IU of Vitamin A, 80mg of Vitamin C, 309mg of Calcium and 452mg of Potassium.

MEDICINAL:

Part	Preparation	Application	Usage
Leaves	Steamed Leaf Poultice	Topical	Ulcers, Stomach Ache, and Sore Throat
Roots	Tea	Ingested	Calm Nerves, Anemia, Kidney Problems & Gout
Flowers	Decoction	Ingested	Laxative

UTILITARIAN:

Salt is critical in long term survival. Boiling the roots or drinking them as a coffee not only tastes fair but also provides the salt needed to allow water to function properly within the body. Due to the latex found in Dandelions, rubber and glues can be made by extracting the white sap from the plant and then letting the water evaporate away from the latex.

CAUTION:

None Known

6. Lambsquarters

Family: Chenopodiaceae	Common Family: Goosefoot
Genus: Chenopodium L.	Common Genus: Goosefoot
Species: Chenopodium album L.	

IDENTIFICATION:
Lambsquarters grows 1-6 feet tall, but they are generally found in the 2 foot range. Vertical red markings are often found on main stem. It often looks dusty due to the white coating on the leaves. Alternate, roughly toothed leaves and shaped similar to a spade.

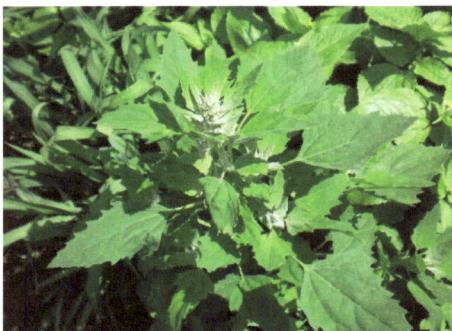

EDIBLE: Leaves, shoots, stems, and flowers are edible. They can be eaten raw, steamed or cooked. 100 grams of Lambsquarters contains 4.2 grams of protein, 309 milligrams of calcium, 72 milligrams of phosphorus, 11,600 international units of vitamin A and 80 milligrams of vitamin C. Seeds can be collected, winnowed and stored for winter and to make bread.

MEDICINAL:

Part	Preparation	Application	Usage
Stems & Leaves	Decoction	Topical	Relieve pain in limbs
Entire Plant	Cold Tea	Ingested	Anti-Diarrheal
Stems & Leaves	Poultice	Topical	Applied to burns
Entire Plant	Decoction	Ingested	Prevent scurvy & clean the blood

UTILITARIAN: Used for a paint on bow & arrows.

CAUTION: None Known

7. Mallow

Family: Malvaceae	Common Family: Mallow
Genus: Malva L.	Common Genus: Mallow
Species: Malva neglecta	

IDENTIFICATION:

Common mallow leaves are alternate, with long petioles, circular to kidney-shaped, and toothed with 7-11 shallow lobes. Short hairs are present on upper and lower leaf surfaces, margins and petioles.

EDIBLE: Both the leaves and the fruit are edible. Cooking is recommended. The fruit looks like cheese wheels. When added to soup, it is a good thickener. I've made chicken and mallow soup that turned out quite tasty. They can be dried and then rehydrated to resemble something similar to rice. It contains very high precursors that are transformed into vitamin-A.

MEDICINAL:

Part	Preparation	Application	Usage
Leaves	Poultice	Topical	Reduce swelling anywhere

UTILITARIAN: None. Chewing fruits are said to keep the mouth moist. While it may make you feel better, it increases water loss, due to respiration, and is therefore not recommended. Due to its mucilaginous properties, like Aloe Vera, it provides good lubrication for the top-rock in a bow-drill fire.

CAUTION: None Known

8. Mullein

Family: Scrophulariaceae	Common Family: Figwort
Genus: Verbascum L.	Common Genus: Mullein
Species: Verbascum thapsus	

IDENTIFICATION:

Mullein is soft and velvet like. Mullein produces a rosette the first year, and the second year, it will generally sprout one vertical, unbranched stem ending in a yellow flower spike. It can grow to over 6 feet tall. The flowers have 5 petals.

EDIBLE: Leaves and flowers can be eaten raw or cooked, however are generally more enjoyably consumed in a tea.

MEDICINAL:

Part	Preparation	Application	Usage
Roots	Made into necklace	Worn by babies	Chewed on for teething
Leaves	Decoction	Ingestion	Taken for colds
Leaves	Smashed	Topical	Apply to swellings, sprains, bruises and cuts
Leaves	Lightly Smashed	Topical	Applied to swollen neck glands, mumps, etc.
Entire plant	Decoction	Topical	Rash reduction
Leaves	Dried or infused	Smoked	Aid for Asthma, cough, and to get rid of bad hiccups
Leaves	Poultice	Topical	Applied to earaches

UTILITARIAN: Mullein is often called "nature's toilet paper." The dried stalks also make exceptional hand-drill spindles. Often used as a ceremonial plant used in a sweat lodge.

CAUTION: None Known

9. Mustard

Family: Brassicaceae	Common Family: Mustard
Genus: Brassica L.	Common Genus: Mustard
Species: Brassica juncea & Brassica rapa L.	

IDENTIFICATION:
Mustard flowers have 4 petals with 6 stamen, 4 are tall and 2 are short. Black mustard is by far my favorite. It grows very tall and if tasted, will be almost wasabi-like. They grow long-slender seed pods. All 3,200 species are edible.

EDIBLE:
Leaves can be eaten raw or cooked. Seeds can be crushed and made into a mustard condiment with the addition of vinegar. Mustard flowers and unopened buds can be eaten raw or cooked. All members of the Brassica genus are edible. 1 cup of mustard contains 215mg of Potassium, 39.2mg of Vitamin C, 1693IU of Vitamin A, and significant amounts of Vitamin K.

MEDICINAL:

Part	Preparation	Application	Usage
Leaves & Stems	Raw or Cooked	Consumed	Taken to increase appetite
Wilted Leaves	Wilted	Topical	Applied to forehead for headache
Leaves	Poultice	Topical	Applied for toothache
Flowers	Dried & ground	Sniffed	Used for head colds
Flowers	Plaster	Topical	Used for colds

UTILITARIAN: None Known

CAUTION:
Mustard can cause burns. Caution should be taken when being applied to the skin.

15

10. Oak

Family: Fagaceae	Common Family: Beech
Genus: Quercus L.	Common Genus: Oak
Species: Many across the USA	

IDENTIFICATION:

If you see acorns, you have found an oak tree. Leaves can vary greatly as there are dozens of oak tree varieties found in the United States. Acorns are generally foraged around the October timeframe. The leaves are alternate, symmetrical and often lobed.

EDIBLE: Acorns are tasty once leached of their bitter tannin. They are nutritionally rich and were a staple for many of the Native Americans. I have collected them for years and had great experiences processing, cooking, and tasting various renditions with my kids and their friends. Leeching the bitter tannins is required.

Hot leaching allows you to use whole nut meat. It does break down the starches, thus is not recommended if you are going to use the flour for noodles, and breads. For hot leaching, slow boil the water and change it out about every half hour. Continue to do this until the meat no longer tastes bitter. To maintain the starch properties, cold leeching is recommended. To cold-leech, crush the nuts as much as possible and cover with at least twice the amount of water to meal. Pour off the water and change 1-2 times a day until the flour is no longer bitter. You can also simply run water over the acorns, that are in a bandana, several times and get a significant amount of the tannins out, making it palatable relatively quickly. Once complete, you can dry or use the flour right away. In 16oz of acorn flour, there is 27.9 grams of protein, 185 grams of carbohydrates, 186mg Calcium, 281mg Magnesium, 358mg Phosphorus, 2445 milligrams of Potassium, and 102 grams of fat.

MEDICINAL:

Part	Preparation	Application	Usage
Bark	Chewed or decoction	Ingested	Mouth sores, chapped skin, throat disinfectant
Bark	Tea	Topical	Douche
Bark	Tea	Ingested	Sooth sore throat
Bark	Tea	Ingested	Antidiarrheal & used for dysentery.
Bark	Decoction	Topical, potentially bathing	Analgesic used for soreness, hemorrhoids, cuts, and sores.

UTILITARIAN: Oak is a great wood for cooking and tools. When the bark is added to water, it creates a black dye. A mordant can be used to help affix the dye to the object.

CAUTION: Livestock may eat excessively and have health issues.

11. Pine

Family: Pinaceae	Common Family: Pine
Genus: Pinus L.	Common Genus: Pine
Species: Many across the USA	

IDENTIFICATION:
Cone-Bearing tree with needle-like leaves. Needles grow in a cluster out of a single point and grow 2, 3 or 5 generally soft needles.

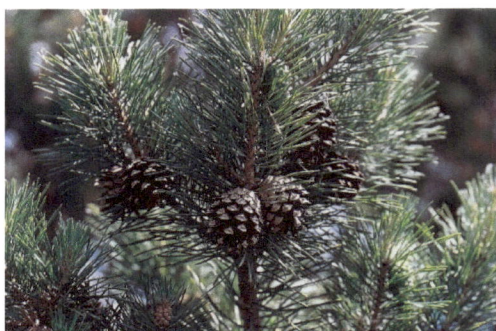

EDIBLE: Pine nuts can be removed from the cones, however the size varies dramatically based on what kind of pine tree it is. Harvest when brown but still closed. Set them off to the side of a fire to have them open up, use a paper bag, or simply cut the cone directly in half to access the seeds. Tea can be made from the needles to make a tasty and vitamin C dense drink. Inner bark is edible however not very palatable.

MEDICINAL:

Part	Preparation	Application	Usage
Leaves	Burnt	Ingested	Used to revive comatose patient
Pitch	Tea	Ingested	Tuberculosis
New Shoots	Decoction	Ingested	Gastrointestinal issues
Pitch	Heated Poultice	Topical	Applied to boils and sores
Inner Bark	Poultice	Topical	Used for deep wounds

UTILITARIAN: Pine is a good wood for a bow-drill friction fire set. Sap and resinous portions of the wood, often referred to as "fatwood", is fantastic for fire starting. Sap with a bit of fiber, such as scat, Thistle or Cattail fluff can be used as a glue to haft arrowheads onto shafts. Some add a bit of wood ash to make a harder adhesive- I prefer not to use ash. Sap can also be used to waterproof canoes or smaller vessels. The boiled roots can be used as cordage. The boughs are great for bedding insulation.

CAUTION: None Known

18

12. Plantain

Family: Plantaginaceae	Common Family: Plantain
Genus: Plantago L.	Common Genus: Plantain
Species: Plantago major	

IDENTIFICATION:

Plantain grows in a rosette pattern with oval to egg-shaped leaves that have 5-7 prominent veins running through the leaf. If pulled apart gently, the veins will pull out from the leaf. Spikes can grow up to 2 feet tall however are generally shorter.

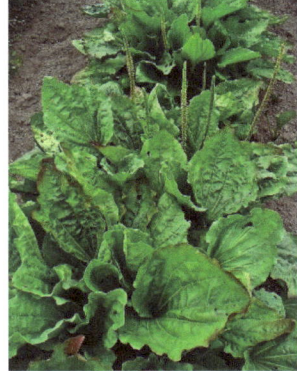

EDIBLE: Leaves can be eaten raw or cooked. The best method found thus far, by Pascal, has been to boil for 3.5 minutes and then quickly submerse in an ice bath.

MEDICINAL:

Part	Preparation	Application	Usage
Leaves	Poultice	Topical	Applied for pain, burns, and wounds, inflammations, snakebites, stings, to draw out splinters, puss, etc.
Seeds	Cooked or raw	Ingested	Facilitate digestion and reduce intestinal inflammation
Roots	Decoction	Ingested	Anti-Diarrheal and good blood medicine.

UTILITARIAN: None Known

CAUTION: None Known

13. Purslane

Family: Portulacaceae	Common Family: Purslane
Genus: Portulaca L.	Common Genus: Purslane
Species: Portulaca oleracea L.	

IDENTIFICATION:

Purslane is a succulent with a thick reddish stem and spoon-like, green leaves. This trailing plant is found everywhere and grows well in poor soil. Purslane is tasty and is often commercially grown. It grows from a central taproot. Leaves grow in a 4-leave, star-type pattern and are smooth and hairless.

EDIBLE: Leaves, stems and flower buds can be eaten raw or cooked. High in Omega-3 fatty acids, they are often cooked with gravies or boiled as greens with meat. In ½ cup, there is 845mg of Potassium, 111mg Calcium, 36mg Vitamin C, and 2257ui Vitamin A.

MEDICINAL:

Part	Preparation	Application	Usage
Leaves & Stems	Decoction	Ingested	Taken for worms
Leaves & Stems	Juice	Topical	Used for Earache
Leaves & Stems	Poultice	Topical	Used for bruises & burns

UTILITARIAN: None Known

CAUTION: Prostrate Spurge is a poisonous look-alike. Remember "Spurge will make you purge." Prostate Spurge exhibits a milky sap, while purslane's is clear.

14. Rose

Family: Rosaceae	Common Family: Rose
Genus: Rosa L.	Common Genus: Rose
Species: Many across the USA	

IDENTIFICATION:

Wild roses generally have 5 petals, a distinctive stamen and a fuzzy center. Hard and sharp spikes are found along the stem. The fruit is often called a rose hip and is a bulbous growth that is red in color. The leaves are often found in groups of 3, growing alternately. Leaves of 3 are often an indicator of a poisonous plant, however the spines clearly indicate the specimen is a rose.

EDIBLE:
Petals and fruit are edible. The fruit is often used for jelly, jams, sauces, soups, syrups and teas. In 100 grams of fruit, there is 123mg Potassium, 22mg of Vitamin C and 339mg of Vitamin A.

MEDICINAL:

Part	Preparation	Application	Usage
Roots	Decoction	Ingested	Cough Medicine
Roots	Tea	Wash	Sore Eyes
Leaves	Poultice	Topical	Stings

UTILITARIAN:
Petals can be dried and used as an air freshener. Leaves can be used in a wash by hunters to mitigate human scent.

CAUTION: None Known

15. Stinging Nettle

Family: Urticaceae	Common Family: Nettle
Genus: Urtica L.	Common Genus: Nettle
Species: Urtica dioica L.	

IDENTIFICATION:
Stinging Nettle has serrated-edged leaves, hairs on the stalk and the leaves grow opposite each other. Varieties grow from short to over 10 feet. The stem is square and hollow. Hairs grow on the bottom of leaves and on the stem.

EDIBLE: All parts can be eaten, however young leaves are best. Nettle also makes a good beer. It reminds me of a sour style beer. I like to add a ½ shot of apple juice that completely cuts the sour and brings out the flavor of the nettle. It is recommended to harvest before they bloom. Nettles can be dried and used as flour. Leaves can be eaten raw or cooked, however if eaten raw, make sure to crush the stinging hairs before consuming. The hairs can be crushed by rolling the leaves in the palms of your hands. I've done this before without issue. Some people with sensitive palms or fingers may get a mild irritation. In 1 cup, there is 6.67 grams of carbohydrates, 6.1 grams fiber, 2.41grams of protein and 3.56 milligrams of salt.

MEDICINAL:

Part	Preparation	Application	Usage
Leaves	Dried & Powdered	Sniffed	Used for bloody nose
Leaves & Stem	None	Whipped Across Skin	Helps with rheumatism
Roots	Decoction	Topical	Used for rheumatism

UTILITARIAN: Stinging nettle has strong fibers that are good for making cordage. To make the cordage you can use a reverse-wrap method. Use gloves or something to cover your hands during harvesting. If you run the stalks over a flame it will singe the hairs and make them no longer sharp enough to pierce the skin. Once this is done, separate the stems down into slender strips. These thin strips can then be used for cordage. The leaves can be rubbed on fishing line to give green color. A decoction of roots was used as a hair wash.

CAUTION: The formic acid in Stinging Nettle hairs can cause a significant rash. It can be removed with soap and water and vigorous scrubbing. Curly dock is known to contain a natural antihistamine that can ease the sensation

16. Stork's Bill

Family: Geraniaceae	Common Family: Geranium
Genus: Erodium L'Hér. ex Aiton	Common Genus: Stork's Bill
Species: Erodium cicutarium	

IDENTIFICATION:
Stork's bill grows 2-20 inches with oppositely-grown leaves out of a basal rosette. The stem is heavily branched and hairy. The fruit is easy to identify with its 5-parted, beak-like, fruit that will coil like a corkscrew as it dries.

EDIBLE: Leaves, base of the fruits and roots are edible. The roots can be chewed like gum.

MEDICINAL:

Part	Preparation	Application	Usage
Leaves	Tea	Ingested	Typhoid fever
Roots	-	Ingested	Help female milk production
Root	Chewed	Ingested	Helps with stomach ache

UTILITARIAN: The entire plant can be used as a green dye, and does not requiring a mordant.

CAUTION: Some say it resembles poison hemlock. Stork's bill has hairy stems, while poison hemlock is not hairy.

17. Sunflower

Family: Asteraceae	Common Family: Aster
Genus: Helianthus L.	Common Genus: Sunflower
Species: Helianthus L	

IDENTIFICATION:

Non-cultivated versions are generally hairy, alternate-leaved and grow prolifically. They typically grow to around 3-feet tall. Flowers are daisy-like with 20-40 florets.

EDIBLE:
All sunflowers produce edible seeds. The seeds are generally either dried and ground to flour or made into cakes with a bit of grease. Nutritional details vary greatly per variety, however the seeds are dense in protein, fat, Phosphorus, Potassium and Vitamin E.

MEDICINAL:

Part	Preparation	Application	Usage
Flowers	Tea	Ingested	Used for chest pains
Entire plant	Poultice	Topical	Applied to snake bites
Leaves	Decoction	Ingested	Fever Reducer

UTILITARIAN: With significant mechanical force, oils can be extracted.

CAUTION: None Known

18. Thistle

Family: Asteraceae	Common Family: Aster
Genus: Cirsium Mill.	Common Genus: Thistle
Species: Cirsium vulgare	

IDENTIFICATION:
Thistles have spiny leaves & stems that are radially symmetrical, with disc flowers that are generally purple, pink, yellow, or white, growing to 2-5 feet tall. The leaves are lobed.

EDIBLE:
The roots can be eaten when young. The stalk can be used raw or cooked, just remove the outer spiny layer. Flowers and the flower hearts can be cooked and enjoyed.

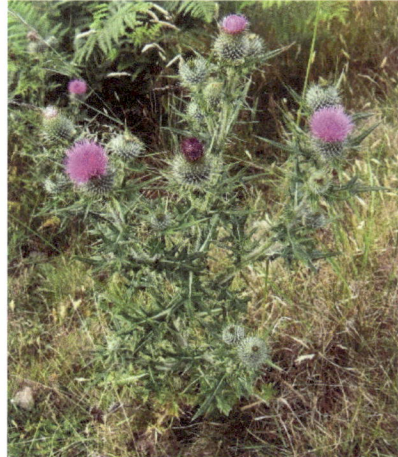

MEDICINAL:

Part	Preparation	Application	Usage
Roots	Poultice	Topical	Used for sore jaw
Whole Plant	Poultice	Topical	Applied to hemorrhoids
Whole Plant	Tea or Steam	Topical	Used for rheumatism

UTILITARIAN: Down from flowers can be used for fish lures. Down is also a good flash tinder for fire.

CAUTION: None Known

19. Willow

Family: Salicaceae	Common Family: Willow
Genus: Salix L.	Common Genus: Willow
Species: Many across the USA	

IDENTIFICATION:

There are an estimated 400 or more varieties of Willow. Generally, the bark is smooth when young and gets gnarled as it ages. The leaves are generally long and lance shaped with a slightly lighter color on the bottom of the leaf. Willows produce catkins that disperse fuzz in springtime as they propagate.

EDIBLE: The inner bark is edible, however not necessarily tasty. In 100g of young Willow leaves, there is 6g protein, 20g carbohydrates, 130mg Calcium, 190mg Vitamin C and 18700iu Vitamin A.

MEDICINAL:

Part	Preparation	Application	Usage
Young leaves, inner bark, or catkins	-	Chewed	Aspirin for headaches, soreness, and swelling
Leaves	Tea	Ingested	Anti-diarrheal
Bark	Tea	Ingested	Used to cause sweating

UTILITARIAN: Willow makes good cordage. The wood is great for a bow-drill set. Relatively light bows (~25-35lbs) can be quickly made with Willow. Granaries were made of willow to store acorns and other foraged goods, because the salicylic acid repels insects. Willow was used as a framework for the dome-shaped shelters the Kumeyaay made called an Ewa.

CAUTION: Caution should be taken if you are allergic to aspirin.

20. Yarrow

Family: Asteraceae	Common Family: Aster
Genus: Achillea	Common Genus: Yarrow
Species: Achillea millefolium L.	

IDENTIFICATION:

Yarrow is a fern-like, strong scented, medium green foliage with long-lasting, white flowers. Flowers form in large compact clusters. It generally is low growing, however it can grow to up to 3 feet tall.

EDIBLE: It has been used in the past to preserve beer. Tea is often made from the leaves and flowers.

MEDICINAL:

Part	Preparation	Application	Usage
Entire Plant	Tea	Ingestion	Remedy for cold
Leaves & Flowers	Decoction	Ingestion	Headache
Leaves	Poultice	Topical	Applied to burns or swelling
Leaves	Tea	Ingested	Break a fever
Tops of leaves	Decoction	Topical	Used for gonorrhea
Leaves	-	Topical	Used to stop bleeding and pack wounds
Roots	Decoction	Ingestion	Stomach Ache
Entire Plant	Dried & Powdered	Topical	Used to stop bleeding

UTILITARIAN: None Known

CAUTION: People known to be allergic to Ragweed or Goldenrod may want to use with caution.

DEFINITIONS OF TERMS USED

Catkin- A catkin is a long, thin, soft flower that hangs on some trees. On Willow trees they bloom into balls of white fuzz.

Decoction- Decoction is a method of extraction by boiling herbal or plant material to dissolve the chemicals from the material, which may include stems, roots, bark and rhizomes. Decoction involves first mashing the plant material to allow for maximum dissolution, and then boiling in water to extract oils, volatile organic compounds and other various chemical substances.

Florets- One of the small flowers making up a composite flower head.

Mordant- A substance, typically an inorganic oxide, which combines with a dye or stain and thereby fixes it in a material.

Petals- Petals are modified leaves that surround the reproductive parts of flowers. They are often brightly colored or unusually shaped to attract pollinators.

Petioles- The petiole is a stalk that attaches a leaf to the plant stem.

Rosette- The rosette is a circular arrangement of leaves or of structures resembling leaves.

Stamen- The male fertilizing organ of a flower, typically consisting of a pollen-containing anther and a filament.

Winnow- To blow a current of air through grain in order to remove the chaf.

IMAGE CREDITS

8 Mullein- AnRo0002
(https://commons.wikimedia.org/wiki/File:20120624Oftersheime
r_Duenen076.jpg), „20120624Oftersheimer Duenen076",
https://creativecommons.org/publicdomain/zero/1.0/legalcode

9 **Mustard-** TeunSpaans
(https://commons.wikimedia.org/wiki/File:Brassica_rapa_plant.j
pg), „Brassica rapa plant",
https://creativecommons.org/licenses/by-sa/3.0/legalcode

10 Oak- anonymous
(https://commons.wikimedia.org/wiki/File:Quercus_suber_g4.jp
g), „Quercus suber g4",
https://creativecommons.org/licenses/by-sa/3.0/legalcode

11 Pine- USDA-NRCS PLANTS Database / Herman, D.E. et al.
1996. North Dakota tree handbook. USDA NRCS ND State Soil
Conservation Committee; NDSU Extension and Western Area
Power Admin., Bismarck, ND.
(https://commons.wikimedia.org/wiki/File:Pinus_sylvestris_bra
nch.jpg), „Pinus sylvestris branch", marked as public domain,
more details on Wikimedia Commons:
https://commons.wikimedia.org/wiki/Template:PD-US

12 Plantain- H. Zell
(https://commons.wikimedia.org/wiki/File:Plantago_major_001.
JPG), „Plantago major 001",
https://creativecommons.org/licenses/by-sa/3.0/legalcode

13 Purslane- Júlio Reis (User:Tintazul)
(https://commons.wikimedia.org/wiki/File:Portulaca_oleracea_s
tems.jpg), „Portulaca oleracea stems",
https://creativecommons.org/licenses/by-sa/2.5/legalcode

14 Rose- anonymous
(https://commons.wikimedia.org/wiki/File:Rosa_rubiginosa_hip
s.jpg), „Rosa rubiginosa hips",
https://creativecommons.org/licenses/by-sa/3.0/legalcode

15 Stinging Nettle- Ben Cody
(https://commons.wikimedia.org/wiki/File:Stinging_Nettles_3.jp
g), „Stinging Nettles 3", marked as public domain, more details on
Wikimedia Commons:
https://commons.wikimedia.org/wiki/Template:PD-self

16 Stork's Bill- Syp
(https://commons.wikimedia.org/wiki/File:Erodium_cicutarium
_flower_and_fruit.JPG), „Erodium cicutarium flower and fruit",
marked as public domain, more details on Wikimedia Commons:
https://commons.wikimedia.org/wiki/Template:PD-self

17 Sunflower- Joe deSousa (Mustang Joe)
(https://commons.wikimedia.org/wiki/File:Helianthus_giganteu
s_(9592721496).jpg), „Helianthus giganteus (9592721496)",
https://creativecommons.org/publicdomain/zero/1.0/legalcode

18- Thistle-   Sciadopitys from UK
(https://commons.wikimedia.org/wiki/File:Cirsium_vulgare_Ha
rthope.jpg), „Cirsium vulgare Harthope",
https://creativecommons.org/licenses/by-sa/2.0/legalcode

19 Willow- Justin Otto
(https://commons.wikimedia.org/wiki/File:Pussy_Willow_Tree_
-_panoramio.jpg), „Pussy Willow Tree - panoramio",
https://creativecommons.org/licenses/by-sa/3.0/legalcode

20 Yarrow- anonymous
(https://commons.wikimedia.org/wiki/File:Achillea_millefolium
_20041012_2574.jpg), „Achillea millefolium 20041012 2574",
https://creativecommons.org/licenses/by-sa/3.0/legalcode

www.ingramcontent.com/pod-product-compliance
Lightning Source LLC
Chambersburg PA
CBHW041227270326
41934CB00004B/191